Whispers from the Heart

Hilary Faith Jones

By the same author:
Awakenings
Waiting for Jesus
The Wonderful Picnic
Milestones

Published by
The Leprosy Mission International
80 Windmill Road, Brentford
Middlesex TW8 0QH, United Kingdom

Edited and distributed by TLM Trading Limited
(address on inside back cover)

First published 2006
© Prayers, Hilary Faith Jones
The copyright for individual photographs is held by
the photographers who are named in the text.

Hilary Faith Jones has asserted her right to be identified as the author of this
work in accordance with the Copyright, Designs and Patents Act 1988.

All rights and subsidiary rights have been granted to
The Leprosy Mission International (see inside back cover for details).

Editorial and Design by Creative Plus Publishing Ltd.
www.creative-plus.co.uk

Printed and bound in Spain by Bookprint, S.L. - Barcelona
A catalogue record for this book is available from the British Library.
ISBN 0 902731 60 2

Be still, and know that I am God...
Psalm 46.10 (NIV)

Jetty on Loch Tay   John Kay

Dedication

For Stephen and Emily Rose,
with all my love.

Preface

When first asked to write a book of prayers based on my favourite Bible texts, I had no idea of the months of work that lay ahead – nor of the joy and the journey of discovery that I was to travel.

Writing these prayers has been such a privilege – one that has drawn my thoughts again and again to the sheer wonder that God, in all his magnificence and glorious wonder, is waiting each day, at every moment, for me to talk with him. And there are so many, many ways to talk with God. For some it is through set prayers, for others through the spontaneous outpouring of the soul; for some, through silence, whereas for others it is through music or the noise of everyday. Some love to focus on a candle or cross, whilst others close their eyes; for some it is at a specific time set aside each day, for others it is a constant directing of thoughts towards God. And so on.

There is no right or wrong way – we each discover what is right for us. As each of us is created differently, so we each find our own way to share with him. That is why these prayers are to be used as is best for you, to share with friends or to say in private.

There are times in one's life when it is very hard to pray, times when one is angry and God becomes the focus of that rage. All I know, is that God does understand – and sometimes, after the storm, comes the stillness, and that may be when God can speak to you. Then there are times when words simply falter. They come no more and the silence is not built upon peace but comes from emptiness and dryness. Then it is helpful to rely on another's prayers, to ease your thoughts back into words again. And occasionally, it seems as if one's prayers reach nowhere. Then it is good to stop for a moment, and maybe change the pattern of the prayer and your prayer habits, and use different words to pray.

I recently attended a week of guided prayer at my church, rather naively assuming I could do my praying as I continued with the daily chores. I was considerably taken aback to discover that I had to be strictly disciplined and set aside a specific half hour each day to pray upon the set passages or prayers. Feeling rather dubious, I set out on my prayer time, carefully writing down thoughts or words that came to me during that time. It was to be one of the most beautiful times of being with God that I could have imagined. And those carefully remembered phrases became the backbone of my prayers for the following months. It was a reminder to me not to slip into the same familiar pattern of prayer that I had become so comfortable with, but to be open to explore new ways and new prayer paths.

And so to the book that lies ahead. When asked to come up with my favourite texts, my main concern was that they would tend to be in the same genre and not sufficiently diverse. Therefore, friends, family and local preachers from the West Bridgford circuit were all requested to help. Over 200 texts poured in – out of which only two were the same. What a tribute to how marvellous the word of God is, in speaking so profoundly to so many people! I tried hard to include texts that I personally found more difficult, especially as they provoked a long series of discussions with God – so I am, in more ways than one, immensely grateful to all who have contributed.

I pray that as you read these prayers, they will become your prayers. And that they may inspire you, challenge you, and bring you ever closer to God, as your journey continues to unfold with him.

Hilary Faith Jones

1 Thessalonians 5:16-18

*Be joyful always; pray continually; give thanks in all
circumstances, for this is God's will for you in Christ Jesus. (NIV)*

O God of such wonder –
it is my utter delight to be able to talk
and walk with you each day;
sometimes I come racing into your presence,
full of news and chatter and excitement;
at other times it is enough simply to sit and be,
gently touching the hem of your robe.
When I do not have the words to speak
then you surround me,
lifting me through the worst.
And when I am in distress,
you understand and slowly walk with me.
So I offer to you my prayers, O Lord,
with all the love in my being –
both those that tumble out loud
and those that are whispered in my heart.

In the name of Christ, Amen.

John 21:12

Jesus said to them, "Come and have breakfast." (NIV)

Help me this day, O Lord,
to speak with the eyes and heart of welcome.

Help me this day, O Lord,
to give of my time to listen.

Help me this day, O Lord,
to share my bread with love.

Help me this day, O Lord,
to learn to receive as well as give.

Help me this day, O Lord,
to be ready.
For this day you will come to me unexpectedly
and I will find myself with you unaware.

O what joys this day will bring –
all praise to you almighty God.

Colossians 1:17

He is before all things, and in him all things hold together. (NIV)

Jesus Christ, holding the world together.
Jesus Christ, holding my life together.

The tentative beginnings of peace between a million different peoples.
The fragile reaching out in trust to new relationships.

The yearning for goodness found all over the world.
The searching for God's will in my life.

The determination to rebuild after horrors have struck.
The steps towards wisdom after wrong decisions.

The natural order and the sequence of seasons.
The growth from childhood into maturity.

The power of love that can bring all people together.
The learning to give and receive that warms the soul.

Jesus Christ, holding the vastness of the world together.
Jesus Christ, holding the infinite possibilities of my life together.

My God and King.
I honour you, rejoice in you and celebrate you throughout my being.

Luke 6:27

"But I say to you that listen, Love your enemies,
do good to those who hate you, bless those who curse you,
pray for those who abuse you." (NRSV)

These words are so hard to do, God,
when everything in human beings longs
for vindication and retribution.
Revenge seems so intrinsic to our nature
that these words come as a terrible shock.
Such a jolt to my thinking.
For they disturb me
and disquiet my soul.

You ask me to reach beyond myself into compassion,
to break away from the inward cycle of revenge
towards a wider vision for humankind,
and to let love govern my thinking.
That most dangerous of all forces
for it changes my perception.

So now, I do not look up at my enemies,
instead I see them face to face
with my arms stretched wide
in the shape of your cross.
And that changes everything.
For it changes me and it changes them.

God of forgiveness,
I'm only just beginning to glimpse the power behind your words.
Please help my faltering steps,
as here and now I offer in prayer to you
the names of those who are against me.

Sunset   David Wright

Jesus – life and light

John 1:4-5

*In him was life, and that life was the light of men.
The light shines in the darkness,
and the darkness has not overcome it. (NIV)*

Light of Christ
be my guide,
illuminating all that I do
and all that I am,
so there are no hidden shadows within.
Christ of light
pour through my thinking this day
so I draw others to you.
And be the vision that will transform
my dreams for tomorrow.

Matthew 3:3

This is he who was spoken of through the prophet Isaiah:
"A voice of one calling in the desert, 'Prepare the way
for the Lord, make straight paths for him.'" (NIV)

O Lord!
Give me the fire of John the Baptist so I know my own convictions
and have the courage to speak out with the fearlessness of youth.
Give me the strength to go alone when companions fall away,
and the sheer tireless energy needed to surmount obstacles.

Give me, like John, that ability to draw people to you
hand in hand with an insight into human nature,
so I know when to disturb and when to give hope.
Give me the passion to inspire others.
And the vision to transform the most barren situation.

And may I strive, like John,
to be the voice that calls people to you,
to live the life that reminds people of you,
and to have the overwhelming love that leads people to your dear Son.
In his name, Amen.

Genesis 3:9

But the LORD God called to the man, "Where are you?" (NIV)

There are times in my life when I hide from you, Lord.
Days when I have had enough,
and do not want to face you –
for I do not want to feel ashamed.
Times when all the subtle innuendos from society
have slipped under my skin
and eaten away at my thoughts,
feeding on fears and prejudices,
until a selfishness has begun to emerge.
And then internally,
I lock my mind firmly
and, foolishly, I shut you out.

But then I hear a voice calling me,
"Where are you?"
and forgotten love comes pouring back.

Forgive me Lord,
for withering my love when I could have shared so much happiness.
Forgive me for hiding from you when I needed you most.
And, thank you,
for you are always there.
And you always welcome me home.

Luke 2:12

This will be a sign to you: You will find a baby wrapped in cloths and lying in a manger. (NIV)

Almighty God

This Christmas,
as commercialism races in and the pressure to buy mounts up,
may I start my journey to give all that I am to you.

This Christmas,
as the world news of wars and disaster wears me down,
may the sign of the star guide my thoughts to you.

This Christmas,
as every day becomes more hectic and I become tighter wrapped
within my own concerns,
may I feel the warmth of the love that surrounds your presence.

And this Christmas,
as I am tempted to rush over the greatest event of all,
may I kneel, just for a moment, beside your crib,
and know that life can never be the same.

This Christmas, Lord,
my heart flutters with expectation
as I open my arms in welcome.

Matthew 13:23

But the one who received the seed that fell on good soil is the man who hears the word and understands it. He produces a crop, yielding a hundred, sixty or thirty times what was sown.
(NIV)

I try so very hard Lord
to believe that good will come
from the small seeds that I sow for your kingdom,
but there are times when I despair.
It seems that there are such barren stretches
when there is no evidence of reconciliation
or signs of new growth.

During these empty months,
it is easy to become disheartened
and to wonder whether what I do is of any value.

Help me Lord
to realize that change rarely happens overnight;
that sometimes the ground needs to be well nourished
before growth can begin;
that what I struggle with now
another may bring to fruition.
For your time plan is much wiser than mine.

And it is enough
for me to know that I do your will.
Lord of such patience
hear my prayer.

Ephesians 3:17-19

And I pray that you, being rooted and established in love, may have power, together with all the saints, to grasp how wide and long and high and deep is the love of Christ, and to know this love that surpasses knowledge – that you may be filled to the measure of all the fullness of God. (NIV)

O Jesus Christ
may my thoughts be deeply rooted within you
my heart full of you
my actions my gift to you.
For you are beyond words –
yet closer than my heartbeat.
In living with you
and in living for you,
may I begin to discover the fullness of God
so I become the glorious person you want me to be.
Amen.

Dandelion   Tony Bagwell

Psalm 51:10

Create in me a clean heart, O God,
and put a new and right Spirit within me. (NRSV)

Eternal God,
as the old year passes and the new unfolds –

Grant me forgiveness for my mistakes
and grace to forgive those who hurt me.

Grant me wisdom to build upon past experience
and unending delight in creating good things.

Grant me peace within my heart
and the strength of faith to nurture others.

Grant me vision to inspire hope
and love to transform each day.

Grant me joy in the gift of this day
and the yearning to live life to the full.

Eternal God, holding time within your hands,
hear this my prayer
as the threshold approaches
heralding your beginnings.

Amen.

Romans 8:38-39

---

*For I am convinced that neither death, nor life, nor angels,
nor rulers, nor things present, nor things to come, nor powers,
nor height, nor depth, nor anything else in all creation, will be
able to separate us from the love of God in Christ Jesus our Lord.
(NRSV)*

O God,
when the darkness seems unbroken,
I shall hold on to these words,
for they hold the eternal truth.

There is *nothing* that can break us away from your love,
nothing that will stop you loving us,
and *nothing* that will turn Christ away from us.
That changes life,
and makes everything worthwhile.

O God!
How I thank you for Christ.
He changes my life and
he makes everything worthwhile.
All praise to you, almighty God.

Rosedale, North York Moors　　　　　　　　　　　　　　　John Kay

In times of sickness

Psalm 130:6

My soul waits for the Lord more than those who watch for the morning... (NRSV)

O Lord Almighty
I feel so ill so terribly weak and vulnerable.
Hold me in your arms I pray, that I may be carried by your strength.
And kneel beside me Lord
so I know that you are with me,
loving me
and surrounding me with healing until the dawn may come.
Hear the prayer of my broken body, Lord.
In the name of Christ, Amen.

Psalm 23:4

Even though I walk through the valley of the shadow of death,
I will fear no evil, for you are with me... (NIV)

There are so many dark valleys Lord.

The desolation of grief
as the world continues to live;
the forced watching from the sidelines
as the grim reality of pain lessens life;
the despair of depression
isolating in its deadness;
the terrible power of fear
as worries and anxieties tighten their grip.

Then I hold tight to these words promised so long ago.

Even in the most endless and deepest of valleys
there you are.
Waiting for me.
Willing to walk quietly beside me
until home is in sight.

Thank you, God,
that there is no darkness
where you cannot be found.
Thank you, God.

Exodus 34:29

*...Moses... was not aware that his face was radiant
because he had spoken with the LORD. (NIV)*

O God, how I love you.
To be in your presence,
to be able to talk and share, to learn to listen,
is a privilege beyond words.
You challenge and disturb me,
inspire and still me,
encourage and love me.
May my face always reflect your glory
and through my love for you
may others catch a glimpse of the joy of Christ.
I ask this in your name.
Amen.

Michaelmas Daisy   Sharon Perry

Matthew 28:7

'He has risen from the dead and is going ahead of you into Galilee.' (NIV)

I love these words, Lord!
They lift my heart when I am burdened
and lighten my fear for tomorrow.

Wherever I go,
I repeat to myself that Jesus has just stepped ahead.

Whenever I am scared at what I have to face,
I recall that the presence of Jesus is already filling the room,
surrounding me with courage.

Whatever I have to do,
I think on Jesus, knowing that he believes in me.

And that enables me to sing with each new dawn
and to look at each new challenge as a further adventure with Christ.

That really helps me God –
thank you!

John 8:12

[Jesus said] "I am the light of the world. Whoever follows me will never walk in darkness, but will have the light of life." (NIV)

O Jesus Christ! Light.
The beginning of all beginnings.
Heralding the new.
Transforming the greyness.
Warming the cold.
Softening the hardness.
Piercing the rigid.
Illuminating the wrong.
Healing the broken.
Inspiring the visionaries.
Filling the empty.
Cleansing the soiled.
Stirring the conscience.
Invigorating the old.
Such life.
O Jesus Christ,
take my humble heart
and fill it with your light.

Psalm 30:5b

...weeping may linger for the night, but joy comes with the morning. (NRSV)

O God, be with me in my darkest times to hold me fast.

O Christ, transform my despair into joy and lead me into the next dawn.

O Holy Spirit, encourage me to live with hope
as life is breathed into each new day.

Thanks be to God. Amen.

Psalm 46:10

Be still, and know that I am God... (NIV)

O Lord!
Life is too exciting to be still!
I want to fill every moment while I'm young –
I want to be at every place at every time;
I want to be at the centre of all that is happening.

O Lord, teach me the gift of stillness,
that I may become more aware of others.

O Lord!
I'm too busy to stop and think.
I feel frazzled and short-tempered
from lack of time and lack of sleep.
How can I possibly be still
when the days are too short and the jobs too many?

O Lord, teach me the grace of stillness,
to enable my life to fall into perspective.

O Lord!
My body is too old to move,
my fingers too swollen to grasp;
I have no choice but to be still
when everything in me yearns to be full of life.

O Lord, teach me the wisdom of your stillness,
so that as others come to me, they will find you, and leave renewed in joy.

In your name, Amen.

Luke 12:7

Indeed, the very hairs of your head are all numbered. (NIV)

Am I really so special Lord?

I look around and seem surrounded
by those who are cleverer,
more beautiful, more sophisticated, more talented.
In comparison,
I am pale and have nothing of worth.
I am simply ordinary.
Just me.

Yet you think I am extraordinarily special.
You are so full of love for me that you know and love me as I am.
That takes my breath away.
And makes me stop a moment
to search my soul for what you can possibly find in me.

Simply knowing that I'm this special to you
changes my perspective on the world
and my perception of myself.
Encourages me to look at others with fresh insight.

I am so special.
Wow!

John 14:6

Jesus answered,
"I am the way and the truth and the life." (NIV)

When I am confused by the complexity of moral decisions,
when I am swept away by current voices,
when I am tempted to live a shallow life,
then I look to you O Christ.
For *you* are the *way*.
The ideal that is my measuring rod,
guiding all that I do and say.

When I look at creation and question,
when I am overwhelmed by clever talk,
when everything in the world seems wrong,
then I look to you O Christ.
For *you* are the *truth*.
And the truth sets free my mind.

When I am uncertain at the crossroads,
when I am lacking in vision,
when I am seeking a purpose for living,
then I look to you O Christ.
For *you* are the *life*.
And because of you, life is abundantly rich,
full of endless possibilities.

Thank you, God, for Christ!

Moel Siabod, Snowdonia

Geraint Wyn Jones

'The LORD watches over you – the LORD is your shade at your right hand;
the sun will not harm you by day, nor the moon by night. The LORD will
keep you from all harm – he will watch over your life.'
Psalm 121:5-7 (NIV)

Amos 5:24

But let justice roll on like a river,
righteousness like a never-failing stream! (NIV)

Lord, help us to speak out
so that our voices carry your truth onto the streets,
to be heard in community centres and town halls,
in the pew and pulpit, the shops and pubs.

Lord, help us to speak out
so that we advocate your justice with dignity and courtesy,
through local papers and national news,
to broadcast on the air and through the media.

Lord, help us to speak out
so that our voices challenge and disturb,
to show that life can be different
and worlds can change.

Lord, help us to speak out.
Show us how to be the light in the darkness,
the inspiration where hope falters
and the meeting place for justice.

Lord, help us to speak out
for you have called us to be your voice,
the voice to set your people free.

John 4:35b

*Do you not say, 'Four months more and then the harvest'?
I tell you, open your eyes and look at the fields!
They are ripe for harvest. (NIV)*

There is such a great yearning to find you, God.
An evident yearning that takes many forms and many shapes
in the restless search for answers and fulfilment.
O God!
Grant me the wisdom to share you
with simple honesty and openness,
to break bread willingly with those I meet
and to live reflecting your wonder.
So my life enables others to catch a glimpse of your glory.

In the name of Christ.
Amen.

Stock Ghyll

Mike Williams

Isaiah 1:17

...learn to do right! Seek justice, encourage the oppressed.
Defend the cause of the fatherless, plead the case of the widow.
(NIV)

Shake me up, Lord!
Let your words disturb my conscience
and shatter my easy complacency.
No longer will I presume that others will shoulder
the mantle of responsibility, for I am called by you.
You embolden me.
And because my heart is yours,
I will stand up! I will speak out!
I will be the voice for those who are unheard.
For I am not alone!
Your son goes before me and smiles me forward.
That's wonderful news, God!

Thistle   John Kay

Isaiah 49:16

---

*"...I can never forget you. I have written your name
on the palms of my hands." (GNB)*

Father God,
I watch the delight in a father's face as his child runs into his arms –
the sheer abundance of joy as each comes to the other
and I am filled with happiness –
for it is a reflection
of your delight in me.
The delight in watching me grow and learn,
the delight when I turn and share the good as well as the bad with you,
the delight in my thoughts and my actions when they are of you.
And your joy in me is such that my name is for ever
on the palms of your hands.
You will always delight in me.

Father God,
that lifts me up
and makes me realise how special I am to you.
I am *your* child now and for eternity
and I want to live to your delight.

How wonderful to be your child – thank you!

Proverbs 13:23

*A poor man's field may produce abundant food,
but injustice sweeps it away. (NIV)*

Lord,
how I am angered by the injustice of trade systems
that enrich the middle man and profit the plentiful,
leaving the poor debt-ridden
while we live in a world that is abundant in resources.

Lord,
teach me not just to talk about fair trade
but to put my anger to good use,
so that I am well informed
and know the real facts
the next time I am tempted to choose the cheapest option;
so I can speak with some knowledge
and put my view forward clearly in discussion;
so I am willing to listen to new ideas and not be defensive.

And Lord,
may I never forget the example set by your son;
so looking to him, I can put my faith into action,
knowing that every pebble causes a ripple.
And through You,
I *can* make a difference in this world.

Leviticus 19:18

*Do not seek revenge or bear a grudge against one of
your people, but love your neighbour as yourself. (NIV)*

O Lord,
to live without vengeance,
this is so hard to do.
I look at my brothers and sisters all over the world
who suffer ongoing humiliation and daily torture
and a question lingers uncomfortably in my mind.
If this was my family being oppressed,
would I have the courage to forgive?

O God,
heart of forgiveness,
unending grace,
teach me how to forgive.
In my society.
And in my life.
To forgive the small slights,
the deliberate hurts
and the underhandedness
that seems to permeate our society.
For without forgiveness,
what use is love?
Two such immense forces
which travel hand in hand together.

I have such a long way to go.
Thank you, God, that you are with me,
to guide my bewildered stumblings.

Doone Valley   John Flude

Revelations 3:20

Here I am! I stand at the door and knock. (NIV)

Still the busyness of my mind, Lord,
for it blocks out the sound of your approach.
Ease the burden of my responsibilities, Lord,
for they deafen the recognition of your voice.
Quieten the troubles in my heart, Lord,
so then I can lift my face to welcome you with all the love in my being.

Micah 6:8b

And what does the LORD require of you?
To act justly and to love mercy
and to walk humbly with your God. (NIV)

O God!
What more do I need?
Your words tell me everything.

May love be behind my thinking,
may it unfold in my words
and be seen through my actions.

May I strive to bring peace,
peace with righteousness,
into the world.

May I burn when injustice is wielded
and be unashamed to stand by your word.

And may I always stay open Lord –
my heart beating quicker as I hear your step.
For to walk with you is my heart's desire
and I ask of nothing else.

God of grace,
I offer you my prayer.

James 1:19

*Everyone should be quick to listen, slow to speak
and slow to become angry... (NIV)*

Teach me to listen, my God.
It is a wonderful gift simply to be still,
letting others talk.
For words are given to enable each of us to unravel our thoughts
and further discover our own path with you.
So teach me not to rush in
but to wait.
For in the waiting something wonderful happens –
as that is when you move,
creating the peace within that enables others to release their worries,
slowing the quick words inside until you have had time to talk with me.
Help me to yearn for and to treasure this gift, O Lord.
To nurture and use it, each day, in all the ways I can,
to bring healing to those I am with.
In the name of Christ,
the greatest listener of all.
Amen.

Autumn Crocus   Sharon Perry

Matthew 6:34

Give your entire attention to what God is doing right now,
and don't get worked up about what may or may not
happen tomorrow. God will help you deal with
whatever hard things come up when the time comes.
(The Message)

Help me to heed your words O Christ,
for worry is a terrible disabler.
There are so many things that press in upon me
and cause me worry in my life,
whether it's health, money or work,
family and friends,
making the right decision at the right time...
the list is endless.
And I have only to look at the world
to become overwhelmed
by the repercussions of government actions
and political decisions.
The worry of it all builds up inside like some awful disease,
eating away at my clarity of vision,
clouding your light in me.
So let me slowly read your words again –
and as I come to you in prayer,
help me to offer all my concerns to you.
And as my faith deepens,
so I shall begin to grow closer to you, my Christ,
and peace will set me free.

Exodus 3:14

God said to Moses, "I am who I am". (NIV)

It is beyond me Lord even to begin to grasp your meaning.
The more I read your words,
the more profound and unfathomable they become.

The more I think upon them,
the greater the possibilities within them emerge.

And it suddenly dawns on me that I am surrounded by mystery,
your mystery.

My heart begins to race
and it is at that moment that I move into deeper faith.

O God of such profound mystery,
guide my frail steps as I tentatively reach out into the unknown.

Roman Wall   Clive Kelly

Mark 15:33

At three o'clock, Jesus groaned out of the depths, crying loudly,
"Eloi, Eloi, lama sabachthani?" which means, "My God, my God,
why have you abandoned me?" (The Message)

Hopelessness fills me.
Words do not touch me.
No-one can comfort me.
I am in the most awful of places.
O God, I need you, now more than ever before but I cannot find you.
The aching of loneliness surrounds me.
Why O why have you abandoned me?
Life does not seem to be worth living.

Then somewhere, deep in the heart of my memory,
I hear another voice cry out.
A voice that was also in this place and that was also overwhelmed by grief.
Again I hear it, breaking with the pain I know.
Somewhere in my unreachableness I am not alone.
Christ is with me.

O thank you God for Jesus.

I cannot touch him nor can I yet feel his presence
for my pain is too great.
But I know that he is there,
sharing my anguish,
grieving with me.

Somehow, just as he surmounted the most awful of chasms,
so I too, with him, will live through this time.
And one day, he will teach me to sing again.

Job 38:4

Where were you when I laid the earth's foundation? (NIV)

O Lord,
forgive the smallness of my vision.
Today, we think ourselves so clever,
so astute, so knowledgeable –
that surely we have become
the greatest achievement of human history?

Please forgive such arrogance, Lord,
for we are looking through eyes that are tunnelled,
forgetting to look up at the wideness of the sky
or down at the miracle of earth.
We have become so bumptious in our self-esteem,
that we have forgotten that real love brings humility;
and we have narrowed our minds
by forgetting to talk with you, Lord.

For it is only through you,
that true insight is revealed.
As it is only through you
that we can realize the gifts that are within.

Forgive me, Lord.
Guide my feet –
and my heart –
in your ways of humbleness,
so I can begin to grow in true knowledge.

Psalm 139:8-10

*If I go up to the heavens, you are there; if I make my bed
in the depths, you are there. If I rise on the wings of the dawn,
if I settle on the far side of the sea, even there your hand
will guide me, your right hand will hold me fast. (NIV)*

O God,
there is no place where I cannot turn to you.
When I stand on the edge of shifting sands
it is my greatest strength to know that you are my rock.
When my heart is sick with fear and I dread the morrow,
what comfort to know that you are ahead of me and I am not alone.
And when I am in some forgotten place and do not remember life,
then you will search and bring me back.

O God.
You stun, amaze, stagger me.
There is no hell, no darkness,
no desolation, no place of abandonment
where I cannot find you.
And that changes life,
emboldening me for the new day.
Thank you my God and my King.

Hebrews 11:8

*By an act of faith, Abraham said yes to God's call to travel
to an unknown place that would become his home.
When he left he had no idea where he was going.
(The Message)*

I am listening Lord, open to hear your call
and ready to respond.
You see, I have too many times ignored your voice
or pretended not to understand
and you have had to gently guide me through my mistakes.
Until finally I have learnt to put my faith in you.
And I know you will never let me down.
I do not know where you will ask me to go
or what I shall encounter.
But I do know that you have called me.
And when I am with you life becomes such an adventure!
So speak, Lord, I am listening.

Snow over Jevington, East Sussex   John Flude

Mark 4:41

"Who then is this, that even the wind and the sea obey him?"
(NRSV)

Almighty Christ
awesome and terrifying
majestic and eternal
omniscient and omnipotent
the alpha and omega
beyond human understanding.

So magnificent and glorious,
yet bending low
to become *my* friend.
O Jesu Christus.
My Lord and my King.
I honour you.

Ephesians 4:15

Instead, speaking the truth in love, we will in all things grow up
into him who is the Head, that is, Christ. (NIV)

As I grow in love, O God,
may my thinking deepen into wisdom,
may my words speak purely of truth,
may my behaviour be always honourable,
may my company bring only joy,
may my presence offer your hope,
may my soul grow with grace,
may my heart be filled with Christ,
and may my face reflect your glory.
In the name of Christ.
Amen.

Psalm 101:2b

I will walk with integrity of heart within my house. (NRSV)

O God,
these words offer such a challenge to us today.
In an age when we skirt around the truth,
clouding the issue by peripheral arguments,
we have lost the forthright clarity of integrity.
Few want to hear the truth spoken in a way that is honest.
And integrity has to start in the home,
built into the foundations of all relationships.
For where else can we learn to be open,
speaking the truth in love,
than with the people we trust?

Yet this yearning for integrity does not flow easily –
for the fear of being insensitive and hurting others
sometimes dilutes our good judgement.

O God.
Grant me the courage to speak out,
even though it may not be what others want to hear.
And Lord,
please grant me humility –
to listen and accept the words of others who strive to guide me.
I offer my prayer in Christ's name.
Amen.

Mark 5:19

"Go home to your family and tell them how much the Lord has done for you, and how he has had mercy on you." (NIV)

O Jesus Christ,
I have so much to rejoice in,
so much to celebrate!
Why is it far easier for me to be weighed down with worries,
rather than living in thankfulness?

Do you know,
I spend so long being overwhelmed by the world's sorrows,
that sometimes I forget to lift my head
and drink in the wonders that surround my life?
And then when I do realize my blessings,
I feel strangely awkward about sharing them with my friends.

Yet life with you is not about keeping goodness bottled inside my smallness,
but of openly sharing and rejoicing in all the gifts that come from you.
So from today I am going to start afresh
and tell my friends of your goodness.
And when they tell me their joys,
I am going to kick my heels and dance in delight for them!

And Lord,
from the bottom of my heart,
I do thank you.

Ecclesiastes 3:1 and 7b

There is a time for everything,
and a season for every activity under heaven...
a time to be silent and a time to speak... (NIV)

O Lord!
How I ponder these words and repeat them to myself over and over.
The trouble is,
I tend to mistake which one I should do.
Sometimes, I confess, I have the feeling I keep silent because it is easier.
And an uncomfortable niggle rebukes me.
At other times,
I speak and simply know I have said the wrong thing and put my foot in it.

O Lord!
It really is so hard to be wise when it is needed!
But I do want to learn.
Help me to put my faith more solidly upon you
and to think about what you would like me to do,
before I make a snap decision that will affect others.
Teach me Lord to really listen to what other people are saying,
so that in time I may start to grasp the truth behind words.

I ask this in your name, Jesus,
for you are the one who understands the gift of speech
and the power of silence.
Amen.

Autumn in Westonbirt Arboretum   Jonathan Leach

Matthew 5:16

"You are the light of the world. A city on a hill cannot be hidden. Neither do people light a lamp and put it under a bowl. Instead they put it on its stand, and it gives light to everyone in the house. In the same way, let your light shine before men, that they may see your good deeds and praise your Father in heaven." (NIV)

Lord Jesus!
Let me catch a little of your radiance
so my whole being becomes transformed by your light.
Then my eyes will discern the truth behind others' actions,
my mind will be filled with all that is good;
my soul will sing of you
and my heart will overflow with love.
And because my thoughts are pure,
my deeds will speak of you
and others will be drawn to your presence.
But particularly I ask that as I look at others
I will learn to find your light in them.
And O how I pray,
that as others look at me,
they may find a face that reflects you, Jesus.
In your name, I offer my prayer.

Isaiah 40:31

...but those who hope in the LORD will renew their strength.
They will soar on wings like eagles; they will run and not grow
weary, they will walk and not be faint. (NIV)

O renewing God,

When everything in me has become worn down,
you breathe hope into my soul.

When my heart is too tired,
your arms lift and carry me through my work.

When I am too weary to push myself further,
your strength keeps me going.

When I lack the courage or the will to persevere,
your vision inspires me.

O God of renewal, how I lean on you
knowing that in your strength
great and wonderful things can happen.

Praise be to you my God.
Amen.

Psalm 102:1

Hear my prayer, O LORD;
let my cry for help come to you. (NIV)

When my words falter
for the sorrow in my own heart is overwhelming,
hear my prayer, O Lord,
and let my cry come to you.

When I can no longer offer compassion
for my own soul is broken,
hear my prayer, O Lord,
and let my cry come to you.

When I am all alone
and do not know whom to talk to,
hear my prayer, O Lord,
and let my cry come to you.

When I am worn out
and have nothing left to give,
hear my prayer, O Lord,
and let my cry come to you.

When I am sick with disappointment
and despair fills me,
hear my prayer, O Lord,
and let my cry come to you.

Through my crying – you will heal me.
From my brokenness – you will summon new life.
Then I will have the courage to face the dawn and see a new future.

Zechariah 9:9

Lo, your king comes to you; triumphant and victorious is he, humble and riding on a donkey. (NRSV)

Where are the heralds,
the golden cherubim and archangels of heavenly hosts?
Where is the fanfare and the royal carpet,
where the guards and the gold and the great people?
I hear only the sound of quiet hooves,
the earthy smell of warm donkey,
the touch of living breath.
And my king is here.
Amongst my folk, my people, my home.
Living, breathing, vibrant.
My king is *here.*
Thanks be to God.

New life

Psalm 34:4-5

I sought the Lord and he answered me and delivered me from all my fears. Look to him and be radiant. (NRSV)

When I was in the very depths
of despair,
so alone that I felt utterly
abandoned,
you came and found me.
Slowly brought me back to being
and gave me hope.
And now my life has begun anew
for I have peace in my heart.

My love for you has no bounds.
How can I thank you for being there
when I needed you most?
I will praise you
by living my life for you –
and letting your love flow through
me to transform the lives of others.
Hallelujah!
What a celebration!

James 1:22

Do not merely listen to the word, and so deceive yourselves.
Do what it says. (NIV)

My faith lives when I put it into action.
So today Lord, with your help...

If my path crosses that of a person I dislike,
I shall try to find something good about them to think upon.

If someone is sharp with me,
I shall try to stand in their shoes and carry their burdens.

If a stranger needs my help,
I shall not be embarrassed but meet their eyes in honesty.

If I am frustrated and want to give up,
I shall think on you and persevere.

If I am asked to give of my time,
I shall try to respond with generosity of spirit.

At the beginning of each day,
I shall offer myself and my actions to you, O God.

And at the close,
I shall give thanks for the opportunities you have given.

And all day I shall pray constantly in my heart with you
looking forward to tomorrow with wondrous anticipation.

John 8:7

---

*"If any one of you is without sin, let him be the first
to throw a stone at her." (NIV)*

Jesus, please forgive me,
for the moments I have lingered behind to share in the gossip,
for when I have tried to shift the blame from myself to another,
for the occasions I have said things that were not strictly true,
for the times when I overstepped the mark
and embroidered the truth to make others look worse than they are.

Christ forgive me.
For these things are not of you.
They stem from a desire to be included, accepted, one of the crowd –
but at the cost of someone else being walked over.

Next time I am tempted to throw a stone,
however tiny it may seem,
let me picture you, Lord, standing beside my intended target.
And let me look into your eyes
and realize that I have no right to judge a brother of yours.
Forgive me Christ and help me grow more like you.

Hestercombe Iris

Tony Bagwell

By taking a long and thoughtful
look at what God has created,
people have always been able to see
what their eyes as such can't see:
eternal power, for instance, and the
mystery of his divine being.
Romans 1:20 (The Message)

Psalm 122:6

Pray for the peace of Jerusalem. (NIV)

Almighty God, this beautiful complex world of yours
seems to be constantly ripped apart by hatred;
such a terrible abuse of power that unleashes untold violence.
I watch the news with a sinking heart.
What hope for peace is there when so many live in oppression, fear, terror?
It is enough to heavy the soul with despair.

But then I hear a very quiet voice whispering in my heart.
Never underestimate the power of God.
For did not violence stretch Christ upon a cross
to have its hold broken three days later?
Was not the overwhelming despair of suffering and grief
transformed into unbelievable joy?
Did not souls that had given up suddenly find a reason to live?

Does not Christ break all tightening bonds that diminish the human spirit?

Push me to think deeper, Lord.
It's no good my standing on the edge, feeling overwhelmed.
Brutality, greed, selfishness, prejudice, emerge relentlessly
within human nature – just as much now as 2000 years ago.
Christ breaks all the evil that binds us.

So next time I feel swamped by the suffering of the world,
I shall visualize the empty cross of the Easter dawn,
and know throughout my soul that I and all of God's creation
are constantly being set free through the power of Christ.
That transforms the world with hope.

Jeremiah 29:11

"For I know the plans I have for you," declares the LORD,
"plans to prosper you and not to harm you,
plans to give you hope and a future." (NIV)

Sometimes it's hard to see the way ahead, Lord.
It seems fraught with difficulties,
or bleakly empty,
or full of compromises.
Everything is simply such hard work,
with no clear idea of where I'm going.
But then I am looking with a restricted vision,
unable to see the larger picture.

Help me to grasp the awesome truth
that I am held in your hand;
that you yearn for good things for me;
that you alone know the potential,
now sleeping, that can be brought to fruition;
and that you will help me become
the magnificent person I am meant to be.
If I could truly grasp this profundity
then *everything* I do has a purpose
and that changes my attitude.

Teach me Lord,
to look at my life,
my relationships, my work
from a wider angle, based on trust in you.
For in you I am held safe.
What a difference that makes!
And it brings with it a shiver of anticipation –
I wonder what discoveries you have in mind for me today, Lord?

John 10:10

I have come that they may have life, and have it to the full.
(NIV)

O Jesus Christ.
You have come to give me an abundance of life.
That means taking risks in my thinking,
learning to question and search.

It means working hard
to realize all that is of worth within me,
all the potential that is waiting.

It means using time wisely,
knowing when to work and when to stop.

It means meeting with other people
to keep my vision beyond myself.

It means standing in someone else's shoes
to learn the meaning of compassion.

It means learning to grow in love
to discover untold beauty surrounding me.

It means being with you,
and willing to follow where you lead.

That's life in abundance.
That's life worth living.
Thank you my wondrous God.

Romans 15:13

---

*May the God of hope fill you with all joy and peace
as you trust in him, so that you may overflow with hope
by the power of the Holy Spirit. (NIV)*

Holy Spirit

Be my teacher
so I can discern the difference between falsehood and truth.

Be my comforter
so I share peace, not brokenness, wherever I go.

Be my nurturer
so I understand the needs of others.

Be my challenger
so I never slide into easy comfort.

Be my inspiration
so I am alert to new ideas and creativity.

And be my guide
so that in seeing life through you, I discover the closeness of God.

Amen.

Matthew 26:40

Then he came to the disciples and found them sleeping; and he said to Peter, 'So, could you not stay awake with me one hour?'
(NRSV)

O God forgive me.
I hear your words echoing through my heart
each time I let someone down.
I always promise to be there for them,
but it is just a grandiose gesture of emptiness
if I am not with them in the small things,
especially in the giving of my time.

Give me the patience, Lord, to be awake,
not just through the immediate urgency,
but in the long months that follow.

Give me the strength, Lord,
not to grow weary with listening to the same issues
but to be consistent in always offering love.

And give me the graciousness, Lord,
to learn that it is not a burden to share others' troubles
but rather a privilege.
And one that brings me closer to you.

I offer you my prayer,
O God who never lets me down.

Matthew 27:51

At that moment the curtain of the temple was torn in two from top to bottom. The earth shook and the rocks split. (NIV)

O Jesus Christ –
what power is this?
By the dying of your body
mankind's veil, hiding God from his people,
is ripped apart.
Death.
Sin.
All ripped apart.
And the power of evil lies shredded,
tattered edges flapping in the wind.
The earth shakes with the impact,
the foundations move.
I too fall to my knees,
my heart thundering with realization.
Everything that hinders people from approaching God
has been destroyed.
Utterly and completely ripped open.
Such is the power of Christ.
All my thoughts, ideologies, doctrines of faith
now take on a different perception.
Through the limp hanging of the torn curtains
light floods the height and depth of the tear.
A light that beckons me forward.
I am awestruck in your presence
yet my heart is racing with delight.
My God and King,
I come to you through the torn darkness
and kneel in adoration.

Sunset, Arran

Barry Knig

Genesis 3:8

Then the man and his wife heard the sound of the LORD God as
he was walking in the garden in the cool of the day... (NIV)

How beautiful, Lord,
that at the eve of the day I should find you –
not in the storm of the city
or in the chaos of the traffic –
but quietly waiting for me in my garden.
I touch you in the gentleness of the breeze.
See you in the startling colours.
Sense you in elusive scents.
Catch you in the mellow sunlight.
Feel you all around me,
surrounding me,
holding me.
Your presence filling my garden
and restoring peace to my soul
before the night falls.

John 21:25

But there are also many other things that Jesus did; if every one of them were written down, I suppose that the world itself could not contain the books that would be written. (NRSV)

How I love you, Lord!
My heart quickens with excitement and joy.
For, as I begin to understand one facet of you, several more are opened up.
Every discovery leads me on to further and deeper revelations.
It's like identifying all the stars in the galaxy,
only to discover that with each and every star,
a further universe lies beyond.
A breathtaking journey – that my mind and soul can only grasp
in fragments.

I am delighted by how much there is to learn of you!
So many questions still to be answered!
How I shall grow within you, my Lord.
But now I catch my breath in wonder –
for this is just the beginning
and such journeys lie ahead!

Theme Index

Bible Verse Index